21st
Century
Skills Library

HEALTHY FOR LIFE
SKATEBOARDING

Jim Fitzpatrick

Cherry Lake Publishing
Ann Arbor, Michigan

Published in the United States of America by Cherry Lake Publishing
Ann Arbor, MI
www.cherrylakepublishing.com

Content Adviser: Thomas Sawyer, EdD, Professor of Recreation and Sports Management, Indiana State University, Terra Haute, Indiana

Photo Credits: Cover and page 1, © Mike McGill/Corbis; page 6, © Steve Boyle/ NewSport/Corbis

Library of Congress Cataloging-in-Publication Data
Fitzpatrick, Jim, 1948-
  Skateboarding / by Jim Fitzpatrick.
    p. cm.
  ISBN-13: 978-1-60279-017-9 (lib. bdg.)   978-1-60279-090-2 (pbk.)
  ISBN-10: 1-60279-017-5 (lib. bdg.)   1-60279-090-6 (pbk.)
1. Skateboarding. I. Title.
  GV859.8.F58 2008
  796.22—dc22   2007003893

Cherry Lake Publishing would like to acknowledge the work of The Partnership for 21st Century Skills. Please visit www.21stcenturyskills.org for more information.

TABLE OF CONTENTS

CHAPTER ONE

WORLDWIDE POPULARITY

Skateboarding has provided thrills and spills to millions of skateboarders for more than 75 years. And whether it's new tricks or a new location to skate, it seems that skateboarders around the world—young and old, boys and girls—are always discovering something fresh and fun about skateboarding. Today's modern skateboard equipment is making the sport safer than ever, and with more public skateparks being built, skateboarders have more opportunities than ever to enjoy their sport.

Skateboarding gives you a different view of the world.

Skateboarders work long and hard perfecting their tricks.

Well before skateboards came on the scene, kids as far back as the 1920s sometimes attempted to build scooters by hand, using boards and roller skates. The result was very similar to a skateboard.

In the 1950s, steel-wheeled skateboards were sold. But skateboarding's first real boost in popularity happened in the early 1960s, when high-performance clay-wheeled skateboards were introduced by Makaha Skateboards in Santa Monica, California. Clay wheels

Learning & Innovation Skills

Some of the world's most accomplished skateboarders collaborated to come up with creative and innovative skating styles. Four important styles have developed:

1. Vert skating, done on ramps and other vertical structures made for skateboarding
2. Street skating, done on benches, ledges, stairs, rails, and other objects found in the "natural" urban environment
3. Freestyle skating, done on flat ground with many tricks, often spontaneously
4. Downhill skating, done down hills

Because of the daring efforts of many skaters the world over, the sport is flying to new highs!

Learning & Innovation Skills

Many innovations have gone into skateboard construction since the days of a simple flat plank of wood. Today's high-performance skateboards are typically made from seven-layer maple plywood. The **deck** is pressure contoured, with a **tail** and **nose** and a **concave** surface. Paul Schmitt is one of the creators of the modern skateboard, and his factories have produced about 10 million of them over the past 25 years. He is so knowledgeable about the process of creating skateboards that skateboarders call him Professor Schmitt. Because of his innovative products, skateboarding is now a much more enjoyable sport!

Some of the world's best skateboarders show off their moves at the X Games.

were a great improvement over steel wheels. And because skateboarding was closely aligned with surfing, its status began to grow. There was even a popular song called "Sidewalk Surfing" that was a hit across the country. In the late 1960s, the first skateboarding contests were introduced, and the sport spread throughout the United States, Europe, and Australia.

By the early 1970s, urethane skateboard wheels were introduced, making skateboarding easier and safer. And with safer equipment, skateboarding developed new levels of performance. Today, thanks to modern decks and wheels, skateboarders can enjoy their sport just about anywhere there's a smooth surface.

If the weather forces you indoors—or if you don't have a skateboard—you can get your kicks from high-tech video games that offer a somewhat realistic skateboarding experience. In addition, millions of television viewers can watch events like the X Games to keep up with what's happening in the world of skateboarding.

Today, there are more than 1,500 public skateparks throughout the United States and hundreds of public skate parks in Europe and Australia. In 2005, more than 10,000 spectators attended the opening of the world's largest skatepark—outside of Shanghai, China! Skateboarding has truly become a worldwide sport.

21st Century Content

The U.S. Consumer Product Safety Commission (CPSC) is a government organization that alerts people to dangerous products. According to the CPSC, in 2001, more than 104,000 people were treated in hospital emergency rooms for skateboarding injuries. Most of the injured were adolescents and young adults. Be sure to wear protective gear and use common sense when skateboarding. That way, you won't become another skateboarding injury statistic!

CHAPTER TWO

THE RIGHT EQUIPMENT

Modern skateboards are the result of decades of refined design and continuing research for the highest-quality materials—all helping to make the sport safer and more enjoyable for everyone. High-performance professional skateboards are available in independent skateboard shops, while less-expensive beginner skateboards are often sold in sporting goods or other types of stores.

Not all skateboard wheels are the same size, shape, or hardness. Try different wheels until you find the type that works the best for you.

Accomplished skateboarders assemble their own equipment to meet the needs of their particular skating style (vert, street, freestyle, or downhill). Although the deck is very important, a skateboard's wheels, **trucks**, **bushings**, and **bearings** are equally important to safety and performance.

Today's skateboard wheels are made from special blends of urethane, a strong plastic. Skateboarders can choose different degrees of hardness for their own type of skateboarding. Softer wheels provide more control, while harder wheels will go faster. Harder wheels are usually for vert skating, while street skaters usually use wheels that are a bit softer.

One important feature that shouldn't be overlooked is the skateboard's wheelbase. The wheelbase is the distance between the truck mounting holes on the deck. Skateboard maker Paul Schmitt recommends a wheelbase of 12 inches (30 centimeters) for anyone under 4 feet (122 cm) tall. As he explains, "Today's skateboards come in different sizes, and a shorter wheelbase is better for

21st Century Content

Skateboarding can be a fun and healthy activity, but it can also be costly. It's important when getting your equipment that you know how to make appropriate economic choices. Choose equipment that you know you will use, that will provide you with enough safety, and that will save you money. If you only go skateboarding occasionally with friends, perhaps renting equipment is right for you. But if you are a serious skateboarder and are interested in improving, purchasing your own board and equipment may be a better choice. Assess your needs, and then be a good consumer and shop around for the best deal before hitting the streets!

shorter skateboarders. They have better control and can maintain better balance." Wheelbase distances run all the way up to 15 inches (38 cm), which is recommended for skateboarders over 6 feet (183 cm) tall.

Under normal conditions, a skateboard deck can last for months, or even longer, and although wheels may wear out more quickly, a pair of trucks can last for years. Professional-quality decks can cost $35–$100; wheels, $7–$10 each; trucks, $20–$60 a pair; bearings, $15–$45 a set; and mounting hardware, less than $10 a set.

Beginner equipment—often appearing to have many of the features of a professional skateboard—can be purchased for less than $100. But it's important to remember that better-quality trucks, bearings, and wheels provide a higher level of safety, especially for the beginner.

Most beginning skateboarders find themselves learning how to balance on their skateboard while rolling forward, typically on a flat, hard surface. The passage to becoming a more accomplished skateboarder usually includes balancing for longer stretches, learning how to push or ride down inclines, turning, and stopping. Back in the days of steel-wheeled or clay-wheeled skateboards, that would have been about all you could expect. But some skateboarders today can do incredibly complex tricks which have developed over the past 25 years.

Most of these skateboarding tricks have developed from one basic trick the **ollie**. First developed by Alan Gelfand in Florida in the 1970s, this trick allows the skateboarder to hop or jump into the air with the board. The trick

A lot of skateboard tricks take you up into the air.

Champion skateboarder Bucky Lasek has been a professional skateboarder for 20 years. His success stems from his own initiative, practicing and setting goals for himself. He began skateboarding in 1985 in Baltimore, Maryland, where his friends built their own backyard ramp. Lasek remembers, "There had been one skatepark in our area, but it had closed right around the time I was first starting to skate. We really didn't have too many places to skateboard, and this ramp in my friend's backyard was really the beginning for me."

Within a few years, Lasek, still a teenager, moved to California, where Tony Hawk became an enormous influence on his skateboarding. Lasek became a member of the famous Bones Brigade skateboard team of Powell Peralta Skateboards, and he was soon touring and appearing at skateboard events around the world. His drive and motivation have made him a worldwide skateboarding phenom!

can be learned indoors on carpeting using a skateboard deck without wheels—a much safer option than trying to learn it on hard surfaces! Tony Hawk, one of the greatest skateboarders of all time, often practices tricks with a truckless skateboard while bouncing on a trampoline. Once skateboarders learn how to ollie, they're usually ready to learn other tricks.

Ollies and other tricks are often taught at skateboarding camps. These camps include training areas where even professional skateboarders can safely attempt the most radical tricks without fear of injury. Campers often discover that their counselors are professional skateboarders, such as Bucky Lasek, Andy MacDonald, Neal Hendrix, or Mike Frazier.

CHAPTER THREE

STAYING SAFE ON YOUR SKATEBOARD

A helmet, knee pads, elbow pads, and wrist guards help protect skateboarders from injury.

Safety equipment, especially for beginning skateboarders, is very important. A helmet is essential for all beginners. Knee and elbow pads are worthwhile, especially for beginners learning to ride on ramps or in a park, where falling safely is an important skill.

Learning how to fall properly is one of the most important skills for a skateboarder to learn. World-famous skateboarder Rodney

Mullen took martial arts classes before learning to skateboard. He realized later that the classes helped him in skateboarding. "Knowing how to do a shoulder roll really helped me," says Mullen, "especially when I was first beginning to skateboard and it seemed like I was falling all the time."

Unlike most traditional sports, skateboarding doesn't have many formal rules. However, most

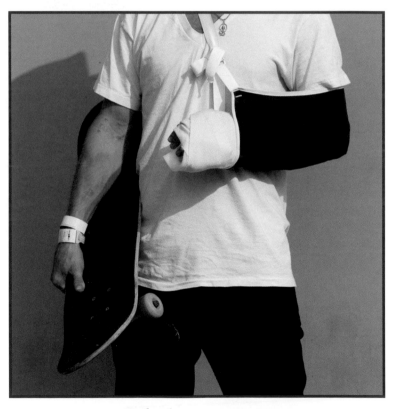

Broken bones are common skateboard injuries.

Skateboarders must pay close attention to one another to prevent accidents.

skateparks have some restrictions, and it's important when skateboarding in specific skateparks to be aware of them.

It's also important to respect skateboarding's unwritten "code." This code has developed over decades and includes rights of way and respect for others. The basic rule involves developing a strong sense of awareness: be aware (be + aware = beware). Pay attention to those around you, and decide whether your movement will prevent someone from doing a run or a trick. If you're not sure, wait until you

Knowing your own limits is important. Skateboarding is not just a physical sport. It is also a mental sport. Skateboarders need to make quick decisions that reflect sound reasoning and judgment. Professional skateboarder Mike Carroll, once said, "I never try a trick I know I can't do. I only do tricks I know I can make!" When skateboarders "make" a trick, it means they do it successfully. Carroll practices skateboarding every day, sometimes for hours at a time. So when he tries a trick, he knows what he needs to do to make it.

At skateparks, everyone learns to wait their turn.

are. Skateboarders who are aware of one another and yield as needed can avoid collisions and other mishaps that could result in injuries.

Skateboarding's code is especially important when you're in skateparks that are overpopulated with eager skateboarders. The code is an informal attempt to have everyone take turns—to "wait in line," even though there's no physical line. Each skateboarder has "rights" and will be granted a turn for a run or a try at a trick. But when that skateboarder falls or fails to make the trick, look out, because the next skateboarder in line will be ready to go. If you fall or don't make your trick, gather yourself and get back in line.

All skateboarders fall sometimes.

Skateboarding is a sport in which communication and collaboration with fellow skaters is extremely important for safety. You must communicate clearly and often with other skaters on the ramps and in the park in order to avoid accidents. Being aware of other skateboarders ensures that everyone stays safe and has fun.

Even Tony Hawk will defer to others who have the right of way when he's skateboarding in a skatepark. He knows the code and would never cut someone off—that is, choose to ride in front of someone who is in a run or trying a trick. The "rules" of skateboarding are somewhat mysterious for beginning skateboarders, but they're just as important as rules in other sports.

This awareness is also important when skateboarding outside of skateparks. The number-one source of catastrophic injuries for skateboarders isn't falling while skateboarding, it's colliding with automobiles! Skateboarders must use their own awareness to protect themselves when choosing a place to skateboard. Be aware when you are on sidewalks or streets; protect yourself and others from injuries that don't need to happen.

CHAPTER FOUR

YOUR SKATEBOARDING ENVIRONMENT

You can do tricks with your skateboard, or you can use it to get from one place to another.

Skateboarding can take place either indoors or outdoors, typically on cement, asphalt, or other hard surfaces. But some people like skateboarding so much that they want to skateboard wherever they go.

Skateparks have ramps, stairs, rails, and other objects skateboarders use to develop their tricks.

As a result, skateboards are now made for surfaces such as grass, dirt, and even ice! There don't seem to be too many places where skateboarding isn't possible.

While the logical place to ride is a public skatepark, not all skateboarders have access to one, so they're faced with finding their own areas to skateboard. In the 1970s, hundreds of privately owned skateparks were built in the United States. Investors across the country realized that there was an opportunity to meet the needs of skateboarders. Despite their success, nearly all of the private parks closed by the late 1980s because owners were afraid of being held responsible for injuries to people using the parks. Skateboarders suddenly found themselves without a place to skateboard, so they returned to the streets. This was their only option.

Consequently, cities were faced with skateboarders on public sidewalks practicing a very different sport than the sidewalk surfing of the 1960s. Modern street skaters are capable of ollieing up onto ledges, planters, benches, and even handrails. Occasionally, property would be damaged by skateboard trucks grinding on the edge of a planter or bench.

21st Century Content

Skateboarders without a skatepark in their community should consider approaching the city government with a proposal to build one. The nonprofit Tony Hawk Foundation was established to assist cities and youth groups with the development of public skateparks. Its Web site (see page 31) is an excellent resource for information on skatepark design, how to present a proposal to a local community, and finding funding for construction. The foundation has donated more than $1.5 million for skateparks in dozens of cities.

Many cities, especially in California, began banning skateboarding within city limits. Suddenly, skateboarding was against the law in many places! "Skateboarding Is Not a Crime" became a favorite slogan of skateboarders. Eventually, they were able to organize themselves and work with lawmakers in California to change liability laws enough so that public skateparks could again be built. Once California's laws were changed, it became easier for other states to adjust their laws. Skateboarders are now often directly responsible for helping to organize the construction of their community's public skateparks.

Even though skateboarding might still be prohibited in some areas of a community—and is typically restricted on private property— there are usually other areas where skateboarders are now welcome. While skateboarding is not a crime, it is important for skateboarders to realize that their sport is noisy, often completely misunderstood by nonskateboarders, and can be destructive to property. If skateboarders haven't been invited onto someone's property, they should look for another location where they're welcome. It's a skateboarder's responsibility to know whether or not an area is appropriate for skateboarding.

CHAPTER FIVE

THE HEALTHY BONUS: BENEFITS OF SKATEBOARDING

Skateboarding is good for the body and the mind.

Skateboarding, despite its risks, is actually one of the healthiest activities anyone can choose. It takes a combination of muscular strength, endurance, and flexibility. Nutritionists and physical trainers agree that regular physical activity is beneficial for everyone. It strengthens your heart and lungs and makes you healthier overall.

Stretching before and after exercise loosens the muscles and helps prevent injury.

Trainers emphasize the need to strengthen the largest muscle groups in order to develop proper fitness. So what better way than skateboarding to exercise your upper leg muscles and have fun at the same time? Remember, you are the engine for your skateboard, and each time you push it forward, you're actually helping your entire body become stronger and healthier. Developing strength and endurance by exercising regularly and for increased amounts of time means you can skate for longer periods of time and more safely. You're more likely to make an injury-causing mistake when you are fatigued.

Even your smaller muscle groups are working when you're skateboarding. Just think how many muscles are involved in maintaining your balance on your skateboard! Your lower leg muscles control the movement of your ankles, feet, and toes. Today's fancy skateboarding tricks call for incredible control and specific movement of the feet and toes. That's why so many skateboarders wear loose shoes; they need to move their toes to help control their skateboard.

Professional skateboarders are serious athletes, and they take good care of their bodies. Before an event, you will see them warming up and stretching, just like other athletes. You should learn from the best and be sure to warm up. Before really getting going, take a quick jog, or skateboard on a level surface at a slower speed. Once your muscles are warm, your movements will come more easily. When you're done for the day, be sure to cool down and stretch. Taking good care of your muscles and increasing your flexibility are a big help in improving your skills.

Consider Mike Carroll's thinking when he says he never tries a trick he knows he can't make. He knows from experience that when he can confidently make a basic trick, he can practice and experiment with a more complex version of that trick. As a street skater, Carroll is constantly

Learning & Innovation Skills

There is another part of your body that gets exercise while skateboarding—your mind! Critical thinking is one of the most important parts of safe and successful skateboarding. (And that's another good reason to wear a helmet: to protect your brain!)

Consider the thinking process of a professional skateboarder such as Bucky Lasek. When he drops in on a vert ramp, he can be traveling at speeds exceeding 35 miles (56 kilometers) per hour. In a split second, he has to decide which trick to attempt and then perform a variety of complex maneuvers. Then he's racing back across the ramp's flat bottom to the other side, where he'll quickly decide on another trick.

One trick after another, all at incredible speeds, make up a vert skater's run. Most vert contests are based on the contestants' ability to make as many complex tricks as possible in a one-minute run.

adjusting his rhythm, speed, and direction as he approaches terrain in a skatepark or other location. His decisions, which he makes in split seconds, are based on his experience and abilities. No one else is telling him what he should do in these moments of decision making. His own critical thinking is directing his success.

Skateboarders are constantly presented with new situations. Those who enjoy strenuous physical activity filled with creative opportunities are the ones who really enjoy skateboarding. That may explain why so many accomplished skateboarders are musicians, artists, and photographers. In fact, many skateboarders enter into creative careers as their skateboarding days become limited.

Critical thinking skills are important to beginning skateboarders, too. From their earliest experiences, skateboarders

*Skateboarders sometimes travel at high speeds,
so they need good concentration.*

are constantly adjusting their body to maintain balance while keeping
their skateboard going in the intended direction. Processing all of the
necessary information keeps a skateboarder's mind active. With each
accomplishment, the skateboarder is ready for another challenge and
another level of achievement.

Like other athletes, skateboarders need to be aware of their body's
nutrition. Because skateboarding can be a serious workout, it's important

21st Century Content

An important part of healthy living is good nutrition. If you're going to be setting athletic goals for yourself, make nutritional goals part of your plan, too. For a healthy body, everyone needs food that has protein, carbohydrates, vitamins, and minerals. Fat is necessary as well, but that is found in meats, cheeses, nuts, and oils, so it's not hard to get plenty of fat in your diet. Try to limit the sugary foods and drinks you consume, and eat mostly whole grains when eating carbohydrates.

Try skateboarding! Who knows what tricks you might come up with?

to stay hydrated. If you ever have the opportunity to attend a professional competition, don't be surprised to see the skateboarders drinking lots of water while consuming bananas and other fruit, as well as high-protein foods to keep their bodies at maximum strength.

Staying healthy is important to professional skateboarders. They depend on their bodies for their livelihood, so they want to do everything they can to avoid injuries and stay healthy. Skateboarding can burn almost 300 calories per hour, and some professionals skateboard four to five hours a day!

Skateboarding's future seems brighter than ever. Skateboard products continue to improve as skateboarders push new limits of performance and accomplishments. Better skateboards have led to more skateboarders, which has led to more public skateparks and more programs that promote skateboarding around the world.

Learning & Innovation Skills

The great thing about skateboarding is being able to use your creativity to come up with your own tricks. But first, you have to learn some of the basics. Once you have these moves down, you'll be ready to go your own way! First, you have to master the ollie, then you can learn to nollie, boardslide, grind, heelflip, and kickflip. Here's how:

nollie: jump while popping the skateboard into the air, while the front foot stomps on the nose and the rear foot is lifted from the tail

boardslide: ollie to a ledge or curb and slide the board along it, then ollie to the ground

grind: ollie to a ledge and slide on the trucks, rather than the board, before ollieing back to the ground

heelflip: spin the board along the nose-tail axis, which you achieve by flicking the skateboard mid-ollie with the back heel; after one spin, you land on the board, wheels down

kickflip: spin the board along the nose-tail axis, which you do by sliding the front foot across the skateboard mid-ollie; after one spin, you land on the board, wheels down

GLOSSARY

bearings (BAIR-ingz) parts that attach to the inside of the wheel, allowing the wheel to spin free on the axle

bushings (BU-shingz) flexible rings that fit into skateboard trucks and provide spring while turning

concave (kon-KAYV) curved in

deck (DEHK) the piece of wood (or plastic or metal) that the rider stands on

nose (NOZE) the front of the deck

ollie (AH-lee) a trick that pops the skateboard into the air by lifting the front foot from the deck while shoving the rear foot down on the tail

tail (TAYL) the back end of the deck which is pressure molded into an upward curve (kicktail) for more control

trucks (TRUKX) axle assemblies that allow the board to turn and that attach the wheels to the deck

FOR MORE INFORMATION

Books

Hawk, Tony, and Sean Mortimer. *Tony Hawk: Professional Skateboarder.* New York: Regan Books, 2002.

Segovia, Patty, and Rebecca Heller. *Skater Girl: A Girl's Guide to Skateboarding.* Berkeley, CA: Ulysses Press, 2007.

Werner, Doug. *Skateboarder's Start-Up: A Beginner's Guide to Skateboarding.* Chula Vista, CA: Tracks Publishing, 2000.

Web Sites

Create a Skate
www.createaskate.org
Learn how to create your own skateboard

International Association of Skateboard Companies
www.skateboardiasc.org
Information from an organization focused on promoting skateboarding

Tony Hawk Foundation
www.tonyhawkfoundation.org
Features information on promoting skateparks in communities

INDEX

ABOUT THE AUTHOR

Jim Fitzpatrick has been an active skateboarder since the steel-wheeled days of the 1950s. Past editor of Transworld's Skateboarding Business, he has been a frequent contributor to skateboard magazines and is the author of Tony Hawk. In 1994, he founded the nonprofit International Association of Skateboard Companies and is currently vice president of USA Skateboarding. A California native, he lives in Santa Barbara, California, where he is head of the Santa Barbara Montessori School.